korean

cooking MADE EASY

Simple Meals in Minutes

by Soon Young Chung

Quick, easy and delicious recipes to make at home.

PERIPLUS EDITIONS

Singapore • Hong Kong • Indonesia

Contents

MAIL ORDER SOURCES

Finding the ingredients for Asian home cooking has become very simple. Most supermarkets carry staples such as soy sauce, fresh ginger and lemongrass. Almost every large metropolitan area has Asian markets serving the local population—just check your local business directory. With the Internet, exotic Asian ingredients and cooking utensils can be easily found online. The following list is a good starting point of online merchants offering a wide variety of goods and services.

http://www.asiafoods.com
http://www.kgrocer.com/
http://www.orientalpantry.com/
http://www.zestyfoodservings.com
http://asianwok.com/
http://www.koamart.com/

Introduction

I have always had a particular fascination and interest in cooking. As a young girl growing up in Korea, I was always helping my mother with one meal preparation or another, so I learned very early the many ways to enjoy nature's gifts. In this book I have included many Korean favorites, to give you a taste of authentic cooking. These include Bulgogi, which is barbecued beef, and is one of the most famous dishes outside Korea, after kimchi. It is cooked at the table on a specially designed griddle and served wrapped in lettuce leaves with vegetables and raw garlic and bean paste.

Bibimbap, which is a very popular dish in Korea, changes from region to region. The basic recipe starts with a layer of rice in a very hot stone bowl. The rice is topped with seasoned stir-fried vegetables such as mushrooms, zucchini, bean sprouts, dried kelp and green onions, and strips of beef cooked with soy sauce, sesame oil and garlic. Red bean paste and a whole raw egg are placed on top to make a sauce that is cooked by the heat of the stone bowl. It is delicious.

Naengmyeon, which is made with buckwheat noodles served cold in a chilled beef broth finished with a dash of hot mustard and the finest slivers of pear, nashi pear or apple, finely cut cucumber and half a hard-boiled egg. The noodles are chewy and very refreshing in summer. This is a real delicacy.

Japchae, a lovely mix of slivers of vegetables such as carrot and green onion with slivers of marinated meat and bean thread noodles, finished with a dash of soy sauce, sesame oil and toasted sesame seeds. It is very popular at holiday dinners and birthday parties.

Gujeolpan, which is served in a nine-section dish, contains mini wheat pancakes in the center section, surrounded by slivers of beef, mushrooms, bean sprouts, finely shredded egg and slivers of vegetables. This elegant starter is eaten by rolling three or four of the fillings with a touch of soy sauce or mustard in a pancake.

Haemul jeon-gol, a seafood hotpot ("*jeon-gol*" actually means stew or casserole) made with assorted seafood, including scallops, clams in their shells, squid, octopus or even crabs or lobsters cooked with ground red chili and vegetables.

Basic Korean Ingredients

Dried chili flakes

Gochugaru

Finger-length
red chilies

Chili peppers called for in this book are fresh finger-length Asian chilies with medium heat. **Dried chili flakes** are made by coarsely crushing sun-dried red chilies. **Korean chili powder** (*gochugaru*) is made by deseeding red chilies that have been dried in the sun, then grinding them to a powder. It is darker in color and coarser than other ground red peppers. This powder is available in Korean food markets. Other ground red chili peppers or flakes can be used, though the amounts should be adjusted to taste as the heat levels vary widely. Some cooks recommend a blend of cayenne pepper and paprika as a substitute 1 teaspoon for each teaspoon of Korean chili powder.

Chinese cabbage, also known as Napa cabbage, has tightly packed white stems and pale green leaves. It has a mild, delicate taste and is a good source of minerals such as calcium, potassium and iron. Chinese cabbage is the basic ingredient in Kimchi (page 10-15) and is also commonly added to many soups. It is available year round in most supermarkets. Choose firm, tightly packed heads with fresh, crisp leaves.

Chrysanthemum leaves are the tender edible leaves of the giant chrysanthemum plant. The serrated leaves have a slightly bitter, grassy flavor. They are often used as a garnish and a flavoring in Korean soups. A more commonly available variety is garland chrysanthemum, known as *tung ho* in Chinese, which is sold in bunches often with roots attached. Store refrigerated and wrapped in paper. Substitute Chinese celery leaves or watercress.

Daikon radishes are large and juicy root vegetables also known as white radishes or giant radishes. The recipes in this book call for Korean daikon radishes (*mu*) which are large and round. Sections of large Japanese daikon radishes can be used instead. Available in most supermarkets, choose firm and heavy radishes without any bruises on them. Scrub or peel the skin before you grate or slice the flesh.

Dried pollack is a small variety of cod usually sold whole and deboned, or in shaved strips. A delicacy in Korea, this dried fish is not salted. It is available from Korean specialty stores. If using salted cod or other types of dried salted fish, slice and soak it overnight to remove as much of the salt as possible, then squeeze dry before using.

Fermented anchovies are made by fermenting salted fresh anchovies—alternate layers of anchovies and salt are placed in a ceramic pot until it is full and the pot is then sealed and left in a cool place for 2–3 months to ferment. Korean fermented anchovies are available in jars, bottles or cans in Korean food stores. Other types of Chinese or Thai fermented fish or fish sauce may be substituted in most recipes.

Fermented shrimp are tiny shrimp that have been salted and left to ferment for 3–4 months. They have a pungent smell and are a popular ingredient in Korea cooking. They are used to make Kimchi (page 10-12), while the juice is often used to flavor other Korean dishes. Look for plastic packets of fermented shrimp in the refrigerated sections of Asian food stores. Other types of fermented shrimp, fish or fish sauce may be substituted in most recipes.

Gingko nuts have a hard shell and are spherical in shape. The Korean variety is small, green and tender on the inside, unlike the common Chinese variety. Shelled white nuts are sold in Asian food stores in two forms—either refrigerated in plastic packets or canned. If using whole unshelled gingko nuts, boil them in water for about 7 minutes, drain and crack open to remove the hard shells. Soak the nuts in water to loosen the skins around them.

Ginseng is a highly prized medicinal root believed to have rejuvenating properties. It is widely cultivated in Korea and used extensively in Korean cooking. As aged ginseng root is very expensive, substitute cheaper, vacuum-packed white ginseng. Another alternative is to use dried ginseng root shavings available from Asian food stores and apothecaries.

Japanese cucumbers are favored in Korean cooking and are much smaller than normal cucumbers. They

Black Chinese or
shiitake mushrooms

Button
mushrooms

Oyster
mushroom

Dried black Chinese
mushrooms

Mushrooms used in Korean cooking include **black Chinese** or **shiitake mushrooms**, **button mushrooms**, **oyster mushrooms** and **enoki mushrooms**. These mushrooms are available fresh, or in dried or canned form from Asian markets. **Dried black Chinese mushrooms** have a stronger flavor than the fresh ones, and are considered to be a bit strong for Korean cuisine. Soak dried mushrooms in hot water for 30 minutes or until soft, then discard the tough stem before using.

have bumpy, thin green skins and are firm and slender. If unavailable, use baby cucumbers with thin skins or pickling gherkins. Cucumbers are usually eaten with the skins intact in Korean cuisine.

Korean hot bean paste (*gochujang*) is a thick, red paste made from rice powder, fermented soybeans, red chili powder and salt, with small amounts of sugar or honey sometimes added. It forms the base for stews and marinades and is also used as a dressing. It has a bold, spicy flavor with a touch of sweetness,

especially in varieties where sugar or honey is added. The paste is usually sold in plastic tubs in Korean markets and can be stored in the refrigerator for months. There is no real substitute for *gochujang*, but the flavor can be approximated by adding red chili powder and a bit of sugar to Japanese miso paste—1 teaspoon chili powder and $1/_2$ teaspoon sugar for each tablespoon of miso.

Korean soybean paste (*doenjang*) is made from fermented soybeans, barley, sugar and salt. It is brown in color, has a salty-sweet

taste and is high in protein. It is often used in soups, stews, sauces and dips. Substitute Japanese miso paste or other fermented soybean pastes with a bit of sugar added.

Watercress stems

Korean watercress (*minari*) is similar to the watercress found in most supermarkets. The Korean variety has a more pungent taste, and only the stems are used in the recipes in this book. If you cannot find it, use regular watercress or fresh cilantro (coriander) stems.

Mung beans are small green beans with a yellow

interior when the skins are removed. These are used in Korean desserts and appetizers. They are available in plastic packets in the dried food sections of most supermarkets.

Nashi pears, also known as Asian or Chinese pears, are brown on the outside with a crisp, translucent flesh inside that is juicy and sweet. They resemble large apples more than pears. This crunchy, fragrant fruit is excellent raw. Apples or regular pears may be substituted.

Persimmons are orange-colored fruits about the size and shape of a tomato. They are native to China and can be found in most Asian food stores. Both the fresh and dried varieties are used in Korean cooking.

Pine nuts used in Korean cooking are the same as those used in Italian cuisine—cream-colored pinecone seeds that are similar in flavor and texture to sunflower or watermelon seeds. When ground and cooked, they impart a creamy flavor and texture to the taste of a dish. In Korean cooking, pine nuts are often crushed and sprinkled over dishes as a slightly crunchy garnish.

Rice wine (*mukgeolli*) is a popular, low alcohol (6–8 percent) beverage, often used to add a slight sweetness to Korean dishes. Unrefined rice wine has a cloudy, slightly milky color and is sometimes called "farmers' brew", as it was once made all over Korea by farmers. For cooking, you can use sake or Chinese rice wine.

Potato starch or bean thread noodles (*dangmyeon*)

Wheat (*somyeon*) noodles

Buckwheat noodles

Udon noodles

Noodles are widely used in Korean cooking. **Sweet potato starch** or **bean thread noodles** (*dangmyeon*) and **wheat noodles** are light and slippery. Thin **wheat noodles** are similar to Japanese or Chinese ramen and are very white in color. **Udon noodles** are soft, thick wheat noodles, and **somyeon** are thin, dried wheat noodles. **Buckwheat noodles** (*naengmyeon*) are similar to Japanese soba and are usually served cold in Korea.

Nori seaweed   Shredded dried seaweed   Dried kelp

Seaweed is a common ingredient in Korean Cooking. **Nori seaweed** is sold as paper-thin, dried, flat square sheets. It is usually shredded and added to soups. It is also available shredded in plastic bags—commonly known as **shredded dried seaweed**—ready for use in soups and vegetable dishes. Look for it in the Japanese sections of Asian food stores. **Dried kelp** (*miyeok*) is a dark green seaweed sold in folded sheets that are much thicker than nori. Wipe the salt off the surface with a damp cloth before using. Do not rinse or wash the kelp as it will lose its flavor. When cooked, the kelp expands into smooth, green sheets and these are used in Korean dishes to add flavoring and color to soup stocks. The kelp should be discarded before serving the dish.

Schizandra berries, known as *omija* in Korean and *wu wei zi* in Chinese, are the small red fruits of the Magnolia vine. These berries, which are said to have five flavors—sweet, sour, salty, bitter and pungent (spicy)—are often used in dried form in traditional Chinese medicine to make tonic drinks and to treat conditions such as insomnia and allergic skin reactions. In Korea, the juice of these berries is used to make the Korean traditional tea Omijacha (page 93), punches and wines. Dried *omija* berries are available in Chinese herbal shops or health food stores.

Sea salt is recommended for pickling and preserving. It is milder in taste and preferred by many chefs over regular salt as it imparts a purer flavor to foods. Sea salt or kosher salt is available in fine or coarse crystals from most supermarkets.

Sesame oil is the nutty-tasting, dark oil pressed from roasted, crushed sesame seeds. It has a strong, nutty flavor that no other oil can match. Sesame oil is used in Korean dishes for its taste and the gloss it gives to the ingredients. Sold in bottles in most super-markets and Asian food stores, it will last for up to a year at room temperature and almost indefinitely in the refrigerator.

Sesame salt is made by grinding dry-roasted white sesame seeds and salt. You can purchase it ready-made, but it is easy to make it your own. To make, heat 4 tablespoons of sesame seeds over low heat in an unoiled skillet until golden and puffed up. Shake the pan during cooking to ensure the seeds cook evenly. When the seeds are light brown, mix in 1 teaspoon of salt, then remove from the pan. When cool, grind the salted seeds to a powder. Store in an airtight container until required.

Sesame seeds are a common garnish in Korean cooking, used to flavor vegetable dishes and marinades. These seeds come in black, white and golden varieties. If bought fresh, they should be dry-roasted before using in Korean dishes. To dry-roast the sesame seeds, heat a skillet over medium heat, add the seeds and toss them continually for 2–3 minutes until they begin to brown, ensuring they are removed from the heat before hey begin to pop and burn.

Shiso leaves, also known as perilla, have a fresh, slightly minty flavor with hints of basil. The Korean variety (*kkaennip*) produces large leaves which are green on one side and light purple on the other. Koreans use the raw leaves to wrap and eat cooked meats. These aromatic leaves are available fresh in plastic packets from Japanese and Korean food stores.

Soy bean sprouts are slightly larger than the usual bean sprouts grown from mung beans that are commonly available in supermarkets. Soybean sprouts take a little longer to cook, have a nutty flavor and are excellent blanched or stir-fried with sesame oil as a side dish. Always try to purchase sprouts fresh as they lose their crisp texture quite quickly. They will keep in the refrigerator, immersed in water, for a few days.

Soy sauce is widely used in Korean cooking. Rich and salty, it takes the place of salt and comes in a wide range of textures and shades. Light Korean soy sauce is less salty than the Japanese and some Chinese varieties. Dark Korean soy sauce is malty but not sweet, with a slightly smoky flavor, and is used for soups. The Japanese or Chinese equivalents work equally well in Korean recipes. Always taste the dish before increasing the amount of soy sauce.

Sticky (glutinous) rice has oval grains and is used almost exclusively for sweets in Korean cooking. It is also available as a powder. Look for it in plastic packets in the rice section of Asian markets.

Sticky rice powder is made from ground sticky (glutinous) rice. This powder is used as a spongy dough for sweet dumplings, cakes, pastries and wrappers. It is sold in plastic packets, but if you cannot find it, just throw some uncooked whole sticky rice grains into a blender and process until it turns to a powder.

Tofu is available in various forms—fresh, dried, pickled and deep-fried. **Silken** or **soft tofu** has a very fine texture, high water content and tends to break easily. **Firm tofu** holds its shape better when cut or cooked and has a stronger, slightly sour taste. **Pressed tofu** (often confusingly labeled as "firm tofu") has much of the moisture extracted and is therefore firmer in texture and excellent for stir-fries. Tofu is available in the refrigerated sections of most supermarkets in packets, blocks, cakes and cylinders.

Chinese Cabbage Kimchi (Baechu Kimchi)

1 Chinese (Napa) cabbage (about 3$^1/_2$ lbs/1$^1/_2$ kg)
1 cup (250 g) sea salt
10 cups (2$^1/_2$ liters) water

Stuffing
10 cloves garlic, peeled
1 in (3 cm) fresh ginger root, peeled and sliced
$^1/_2$ onion, peeled and sliced

Makes about 4 cups

3–4 red chili peppers, deseeded
1 medium daikon radish (10 oz/300 g), peeled and sliced into matchsticks
1–2 green onions, cut into short lengths
6–8 Korean watercress stems (*minari*), cut into short lengths

4 tablespoons fermented shrimp or fish sauce
4 tablespoons fermented anchovies
4–5 tablespoons Korean chili powder
2 tablespoons sticky (glutinous) rice powder dissolved in $^3/_4$ cup (185 ml) water
2 tablespoons sugar (optional)

1 Remove and discard the outer leaves of the cabbage, and halve it lengthwise. Combine the salt and water in a large container and stir until the salt is dissolved. Soak the cabbage halves in the salt water for 3–4 hours with a weight on top of the leaves to keep them submerged. Remove the cabbage from the salted water, rinse and squeeze out the excess water.

2 To prepare the Stuffing, process the garlic, ginger, onion, chili and $1/_2$ cup (125 ml) of water to a smooth paste in a blender. Combine the vegetables and processed paste in a large bowl.

3 Add all the other Stuffing ingredients and toss until well blended. Set aside for 10 minutes.

4 Using your fingers, separate the leaves of the cabbage halves and spoon some of the Stuffing between each leaf, ensuring all the leaves are well coated on both sides. Place the stuffed cabbage in an airtight container, cover and set aside in a cool place for 2–3 days to mature, then chill in the refrigerator before using. Store any unused kimchi in the refrigerator for up to 1 week.

White Kimchi (Baek Kimchi)

1 Chinese (Napa) cabbage (about 3$^1/_2$ lbs/1$^1/_2$ kg)
1 cup (250 g) sea salt
10 cups (2$^1/_2$ liters) beef stock or water

Stuffing
3 oz (90 g) daikon radish, peeled and sliced into thin strips
2 green onions, cut into short lengths
6–8 Korean watercress stems (*minari*), cut into short lengths
2 oz (60 g) mustard leaves, cut into short lengths
1 pear (preferably nashi), peeled, cored and sliced into strips
5 chestnuts, sliced
5 dried pitted dates
5 dried black Chinese mushrooms, soaked until soft, rinsed well and squeezed dry, stems trimmed, caps sliced into strips
5 cloves garlic, minced
1 teaspoon grated fresh ginger root
1 red chili pepper, deseeded and cut into thin strips (optional)
4 tablespoons fermented shrimp or fish sauce
2 tablespoons sugar
2 cups (500 ml) water

1 Remove and discard the outer leaves of the cabbage, and halve it lengthwise. Combine the salt and beef stock or water in a large container and stir until the salt is dissolved. Soak the cabbage halves in the salted stock or water for 6–8 hours with a weight on top of the leaves to keep them submerged. Remove the cabbage from the container, rinse and shake off the excess water.
2 To prepare the Stuffing, combine all the ingredients in a large bowl and mix thoroughly.
3 Using your fingers, separate the leaves of the cabbage halves and spoon some of the Stuffing between each leaf, ensuring all the leaves are well coated on both sides. Place the stuffed cabbage in an airtight container, cover and set aside in a cool place for 2–3 days to mature, then chill in the refrigerator before using. Store any unused kimchi in the refrigerator.

Makes about 4 cups

Watery Kimchi

1 lb (500 g) Chinese (Napa) cabbage, sliced
1 medium daikon radish (8 oz/250 g), peeled and sliced into strips
4 tablespoons sea salt
8 cups (2 liters) water
2$^1/_2$ tablespoons Korean chili powder
1 clove garlic, minced
1 teaspoon grated fresh ginger root
2 teaspoons sugar, or to taste
1 teaspoon salt, or to taste
6–8 Korean watercress stems (*minari*), cut into short lengths
$^1/_2$ nashi or other firm pear, peeled, cored and sliced
1 onion, sliced
2 green onions, white part only, cut into short lengths
1 red chili pepper, deseeded and cut into thin strips

1 Place the cabbage and radish in a bowl and sprinkle with the salt. Set aside for 15–20 minutes, tossing occasionally, then rinse well and drain.

2 Combine the water and chili powder in a pot and mix well, then strain into a large airtight container, discarding any undissolved chili powder. Add the garlic, ginger, sugar and salt to the chili water, and mix until the sugar is dissolved, then stir in the radish, cabbage and all the other ingredients. Mix thoroughly.

3 Cover the container tightly and leave the kimchi in a cool place for 2–3 days to mature before using. Store the unused portion in the refrigerator for about 5 days.

Makes about 12 cups (3 liters)

Cucumber Kimchi

5 Japanese cucumbers
3 tablespoons sea salt

Stuffing
2 green onions, minced
  (optional)
$1/2$ pear (preferably
  nashi), peeled, cored
  and minced
2 cloves garlic, minced
1 teaspoon grated fresh
  ginger root
2 tablespoons fermented
  shrimp (optional)
2 tablespoons Korean
  chili powder
2 teaspoons sugar

1 Scrub the cucumbers, then cut off and discard the
top and bottom $1/2$ in (1 cm) of the cucumbers. Half
each cucumber and make two 1-in (2-cm) slits, at
90-degree angles to each other, down each half of the
cucumbers. Rub the salt evenly over the cucumber
halves and set aside for 2 hours.
2 Combine the Stuffing ingredients in a bowl and
mix well.
3 Rinse the cucumber halves, then gently squeeze out
the excess water from them and dry with paper towels.
Press the Stuffing into each slit of the cucumber halves.
4 Place the stuffed cucumbers in a container and
cover tightly, then set aside in a cool place overnight.
Serve chilled within 2–3 days when the cucumber is
still crisp.

Serves 4

Simple Beef and Vegetable Appetizer

5 oz (150 g) beef, sliced
into strips
Oil, for frying
1 nori sheet, cut into thin
strips
6–8 Korean watercress
stems (*minari*), cut into
short lengths
2 cups (100 g) bean
sprouts, tails trimmed,
blanched for 1 minute

Marinade
1 tablespoon soy sauce
2 teaspoons sugar
1 teaspoon minced garlic
1 teaspoon sesame oil
1 teaspoon sesame paste
Pinch of freshly ground
black pepper

Egg Strips
1 egg, white and yolk
separated

Dressing
1$^1/_2$ tablespoons soy
sauce
1$^1/_2$ tablespoons white
vinegar
1 teaspoon sugar

Serves 4

1 Combine the Marinade ingredients in a bowl and marinate the beef slices in it for
10-15 minutes. In a nonstick skillet, sauté the beef strips in 1 tablespoon of oil over
medium heat for 3–5 minutes until cooked through. Set aside.
2 Prepare the Egg Strips as described on page 47.
3 Combine the Dressing ingredients in a serving bowl and mix well. Arrange the
beef, nori, watercress stems, bean sprouts and Egg Strips on a serving platter and
serve with the bowl of Dressing on the side.

Seasoned Vegetables (Namul)

Spinach
2 cups (500 ml) water
Pinch of salt
10 oz (300 g) fresh
  spinach, roots removed,
  leaves and stems cut
  into short lengths
1 tablespoon minced
  green onion
1 tablespoon crushed
  garlic paste
1 1/2 tablespoons soy
  sauce
1 teaspoon sesame oil
2 teaspoons sesame paste

Mushrooms
10 fresh or dried black
  Chinese mushrooms
2 teaspoons crushed
  garlic paste
1 tablespoon minced
  green onion
1/2 teaspoon salt
2 teaspoons soy sauce
1 teaspoon sesame paste
1 teaspoon sesame oil
Pinch of freshly ground
  black pepper
1 tablespoon oil

Green Bell Pepper
1 tablespoon oil
2 teaspoons crushed
  garlic paste
1 green bell pepper,
  deseeded, cut into very
  thin strips
1 tablespoon minced
  green onion
1/2 teaspoon salt, or to
  taste
1 teaspoon sesame oil
2 teaspoons sesame
  paste

1 Prepare the Spinach first by bringing the water and salt to a boil over high heat in a saucepan. Blanch the spinach for 1–2 minutes and remove from the heat. Rinse the blanched spinach in cold water and drain well. Squeeze out the excess water from the spinach. Combine the spinach with all the other ingredients in a bowl and mix until well coated. Set aside.

2 To prepare the Mushrooms, return the salted water to a boil over high heat and blanch the fresh mushrooms for 15 seconds or the dried mushrooms for 3-5 minutes, adding more water as needed. Remove from the heat, rinse in cold water and drain well. Squeeze out the excess water from the mushrooms. Remove and discard the stems, then thinly slice the caps.

3 In a bowl, combine the mushroom slices with all the other ingredients, except the oil, and mix well. Heat the oil in a skillet over medium heat and sauté the mushroom mixture for 2–3 minutes. Remove from the heat and set aside.

4 To cook the Green Bell Pepper, heat the oil in a skillet over medium heat and sauté the garlic until golden and fragrant, about 30 seconds. Add all the other ingredients, sauté for 1 minute and remove from the heat.

5 Arrange the vegetables in separate piles on a serving platter and serve as a side dish with other main dishes and steamed rice.

For variations, you can use other vegetables you like. The photo on the right shows a different combination of spinach, Chinese bellflower root and fernbrake.

Serves 4

Stuffed Zucchini (Hobakseon)

1 medium zucchini
2 tablespoons salt
3 cups (750 ml) water
5 oz (150 g) ground beef
3 dried black Chinese
  mushrooms, soaked
  until soft, rinsed well
  and squeezed dry,
  stems trimmed, caps
  finely chopped
$1^1/_2$ tablespoons oil
1 tablespoon soy sauce
1 tablespoon sugar
$^1/_4$ cup (60 ml) beef
  stock
Red chili strips, to garnish

Marinade
2 teaspoons soy sauce
1 teaspoon sugar
$1^1/_2$ tablespoons minced
  green onion
2 teaspoons crushed
  garlic paste
1 teaspoon sesame oil
1 teaspoon sesame paste
Freshly ground black
  pepper, to taste

Egg Strips
1 egg, white and yolk
  separated
Oil, for frying

1 Slice the zucchini into 2-in (5-cm) sections. Make a well about $^3/_4$ in (2 cm) deep at one end of each zucchini section. Dissolve the salt in the water and soak the zucchini for about 30 minutes.

2 Combine the Marinade ingredients in a bowl and mix well. Add the beef and mushroom to the Marinade, mix until well blended and allow to marinate for 20–30 minutes. Heat the oil in a skillet over high heat and sauté the marinated beef and mushroom for 2–3 minutes. Remove from the heat and set aside.

3 Prepare the Egg Strips as described on page 47.

4 Remove the zucchini from the soaking water. Gently squeeze out the excess water from them and dry with paper towels. Fill the well of each zucchini section with the beef and mushroom mixture, pressing in firmly. Set aside.

5 Bring the soy sauce, sugar and beef stock to a boil over medium heat in a saucepan. Add the stuffed zucchini and simmer uncovered for 1 minute. Reduce the heat to low and continue to simmer for 2-3 minutes, spooning the sauce over the stuffed zucchini from time to time. Removed from the heat and transfer to serving platters. Top the stuffed zucchini with the Egg Strips and garnish with chili strips.

Serves 4

Beef Strips in
Lettuce Leaves (Bulgogi)

1 lb (500 g) beef sirloin
1 nashi pear, peeled
1 1/2 teaspoons rice wine
1 onion, peeled
1 carrot, peeled
1 green bell pepper
Lettuce leaves, to serve

Marinade
1 1/2 teaspoons minced
  garlic
1 tablespoon dry-roasted
  sesame seeds (optional)
1 1/2 teaspoons soy sauce
1 tablespoon sugar

1 1/2 teaspoons sesame oil
Freshly ground black
  pepper, to taste

Serves 4

1 Slice the beef into long, thin strips. Grate the pear, then press to obtain juice. In a bowl, combine the beef, pear juice and rice wine and mix well, then set aside for 30 minutes to marinate.

2 Mix the Marinade ingredients in another bowl. Add the seasoned beef and mix until well coated. Cover and allow to marinate in the refrigerator for 2–3 hours.

3 Slice the onion and carrot, deseed and cut the bell pepper into pieces. Arrange the raw vegetables on serving platters.

4 Grill or stir-fry the marinated beef until cooked. Serve hot. Eat wrapped in lettuce leaf parcels with vegetables.

For added bite, accompany the vegetables with a dipping sauce of red chili and soybean paste. Traditionally, beef Bulgogi is made with wide, thin shavings of beef. But here, we use the most common beef cut available in Western markets.

Stuffed Mushrooms (Pyogojeon)

12 dried black Chinese
mushrooms
4 oz (125 g) ground beef
$1/_4$ cake (2 oz/60 g) soft
tofu, drained and
mashed with a fork
2 tablespoons flour
1 egg, beaten
Oil, for frying

Beef Seasoning
1 tablespoon soy sauce
$1^1/_2$ tablespoons sugar
2 teaspoons minced
green onion
1 teaspoon crushed garlic
paste
1 teaspoon sesame oil
1 teaspoon sesame paste
Pinch of freshly ground
black pepper

Dipping Sauce
2 tablespoons soy sauce
1 tablespoon water
1 tablespoon vinegar
1 tablespoon dry-roasted,
ground pine nuts

1 Soak the mushrooms in hot water until soft,
20–30 minutes. Rinse and drain the mushrooms,
then squeeze out the excess moisture. Remove and
discard the stems from the mushrooms and set aside.
2 Combine the Beef Seasoning ingredients in a bowl
and mix well. Add the beef and tofu and mix until
well blended.
3 To stuff the mushrooms, lightly coat the inside of
each mushroom cap with a little bit of the flour, then
fill it with the beef mixture, pressing in firmly. Set aside.
4 Prepare the Dipping Sauce by combining all the
ingredients in a bowl and mix well.
5 Heat 1 tablespoon of oil over high heat in a skillet
until hot. Handling a few at a time, lightly dust the
stuffed mushrooms with flour, then dip them in the
beaten egg and fry for about 2 minutes on the stuffed
side until golden brown. Turn them over and continue
to fry the other side for 1 minute, then remove from
the heat. Transfer to a serving platter and serve hot
with a bowl of the Dipping Sauce on the side.

Dipping the stuffed mushrooms in the beaten egg will
prevent them from absorbing too much oil when frying.

Serves 4

Tangy Squid Kebabs

3–4 medium squid bodies (about 8 oz/250 g in total), cut open and cleaned
2 green bell peppers, cored and deseeded
12 bamboo skewers, soaked in water for 1 hour before using
Oil, for frying

Seasoning
4 tablespoons Korean hot bean paste (*gochujang*)
2 tablespoons sugar
2 tablespoons crushed garlic paste
2 green onions, minced
1 teaspoon ginger juice (pressed from grated fresh ginger root)
1 teaspoon sesame paste
1 teaspoon sesame oil

1 Using the tip of a knife, score the surface of the squid in a crisscross pattern to prevent it from over-curling during cooking. Bring a saucepan of water to a boil and poach the squid until it just begins to curl, 2–3 minutes. Remove from the heat, drain and slice the squid into $^3/_4$ x $2^1/_2$-in (2 x 6-cm) strips. Slice the bell pepper into strips roughly the same size.
2 Combine the Seasoning ingredients in a bowl and mix well.
3 Thread the squid, alternating with the bell pepper strips, onto the skewers. Brush each skewer with the Seasoning, coating both sides well.
4 Heat a little oil in a nonstick skillet until hot and fry the skewers for about 1 minute on each side, being careful not to burn them. Alternatively, grill in a pan grill or oven. Serve immediately with steamed rice.

Serves 2–4

Spring Roll Appetizer Plate (Gujeolpan)

4 oz (125 g) beef, sliced into very thin strips
5 dried black Chinese mushrooms, soaked until soft, rinsed well and squeezed dry, stems trimmed, caps sliced
Oil, for frying
5 oz (150 g) button mushrooms, thinly sliced
1 Japanese cucumber, peeled and cut into matchsticks
1 carrot, peeled and cut into matchsticks

$1^1/_2$ cups (150 g) bean sprouts, tails trimmed
Sesame oil
Salt and ground white pepper, to taste

Marinade
2 tablespoons soy sauce
1 tablespoon sugar
2 tablespoons minced green onion
1 tablespoon minced garlic
2 teaspoons sesame oil
2 teaspoons sesame paste
Freshly ground black pepper, to taste

Egg Strips
3 eggs, white and yolk separated

Crepes
1 cup (150 g) flour, sifted
$1/_2$ teaspoon salt
$1^1/_4$ cups (300 ml) water
1 teaspoon dry-roasted pine nuts, halved

Dressing
3 tablespoons soy sauce
$4^1/_2$ teaspoons vinegar
1 tablespoon water

1 Combine the Marinade ingredients in a bowl and mix well. Pour equally into 2 bowls and place the beef strips in one and the mushroom in the other. Mix thoroughly and marinate the beef and mushrooms for at least 20 minutes.
2 Heat 1 tablespoon of oil in a nonstick skillet and sauté the beef over high heat for 2–3 minutes. Remove and drain on paper towels. Clean the pan, heat 1 tablespoon of oil and sauté the mushroom for 1 minute, then repeat with the button mushroom in the same manner. Remove from the heat and drain on paper towels.
3 To prepare the vegetables, soak the cucumber in lightly salted water for 5 minutes, then drain and squeeze out any excess water. In a skillet, sauté the cucumber in a little oil for 30 seconds, then drain on paper towels. Clean the pan and sauté the carrot for 1 minute. Blanch the bean sprouts in boiling water for about 30 seconds, then drain and squeeze out any excess water. Season the blanched bean sprouts with a few drops of sesame oil and a pinch of salt and pepper. Set the vegetables aside.
4 Prepare the Egg Strips as described on page 47 and set aside.
5 To make the Crepes, mix all the ingredients into a batter. Lightly grease a nonstick skillet and heat over medium heat. Pour in 1 tablespoon of the batter and cook until off-white (do not brown), about 1 minute. Turn the pancake over and cook the other side for another minute. Remove from the heat and sprinkle with some pine nut halves. Continue to make the Crepes in the same manner with the remaining batter. Stack the Crepes in the center of a *gujeolpan* dish or a large serving platter.
6 Combine the Dressing ingredients in a bowl and mix well.
7 Arrange the fillings around the Crepes and serve with bowls of Dressing on the side. Invite your guests to spread a little Dressing on the crepe, top with the fillings of their choice and roll it up before eating it.

Serves 4

Beef Salad with Pear and Pine Nut Dressing

8 oz (250 g) beef
1 stalk celery, sliced diagonally
1 Japanese cucumber, halved and sliced diagonally
$^1/_2$ pear (preferably nashi), peeled, cored and sliced,
   sprinkled with a little sugar to prevent browning
1 red radish, halved and thinly sliced
2 teaspoons vinegar
1 teaspoon salt
$^1/_2$ teaspoon hot prepared mustard
Celery leaves, to garnish

Pine Nut Dressing
$^1/_3$ cup (35 g) pine nuts
2 tablespoons milk
$^1/_2$ teaspoon salt, or to taste

1 In a large saucepan, cover the beef with water and
bring to a boil over medium heat, then simmer
uncovered until tender, about 30 minutes. Remove
the beef from the pan and wrap it in a clean cloth.
Place a heavy object on top of the beef for about
2 hours to firm it, then slice the beef into $^1/_2$ in (1 cm)
thick pieces. Set aside.
2 Prepare the Pine Nut Dressing by processing all the
ingredients to a smooth paste in a blender. Set aside.
3 Combine all the ingredients, except the garnish, in a
large bowl. Pour the dressing over and toss well.
Transfer to a bed of celery leaves on a serving platter
and serve chilled.

Serves 4

Sliced Chicken Kebabs (Daksanjeok)

1 lb (500 g) boneless
  chicken breasts
Salt and freshly ground
  black pepper
2 tablespoons oil
Sesame oil, to taste
2–3 green onions, cut
  into 1^1/$_2$-in (4-cm)
  lengths
16 bamboo skewers
Red chili pepper strips, to
  garnish

Sauce
5 tablespoons soy sauce
2 tablespoons sugar
1 tablespoon malt liquid
  (see note)
1 tablespoon ginger juice
  (pressed from grated
  fresh ginger root)
1 tablespoon rice wine
^{1}/$_4$ cup (60 ml) water

Egg Strips
1 egg, white and yolk
  separated
Oil, for frying

Serves 4

1 Clean the chicken breasts and pat dry with paper towels. Place each between sheets of plastic wrap and pound with a mallet to about ^{1}/$_4$ in (6 mm) thick. Cut the edges of each chicken breast with a knife tip every 2 in (5 cm) or so to prevent it from curling and shrinking when cooked, then sprinkle with some salt and pepper.

2 Heat the oil in a skillet until very hot but not smoking and fry the chicken breasts for about 2 minutes on each side. Remove from the heat and set aside.

3 Bring the Sauce ingredients to a boil in a saucepan. Reduce the heat to low and simmer uncovered until the Sauce is thick, 3–5 minutes. Add the chicken breasts and continue to simmer for 10–15 minutes. Remove from the heat.

4 Remove the chicken from the Sauce and slice it into 1^1/$_2$ in (4 cm) long strips. Sprinkle the chicken strips with sesame oil and set aside to cool. Transfer the Sauce to a serving bowl.

5 Prepare the Egg Strips as described on page 47.

6 Thread the chicken strips onto skewers, alternating with the green onion lengths. Arrange the skewers on serving platters, top with the Egg Strips and chili strips, and serve with a bowl of Sauce on the side.

Malt liquid or malt syrup is the syrup made by dissolving the sugar from malted barley and removing much of the water. It is sold in jars, bottles or cans in the supermarkets.

Pork and Kimchi Pancake Appetizer

1 cup (200 g) dried mung
  beans
1 cup (250 ml) water
3 tablespoons sticky
  (glutinous) rice powder
1/2 onion, peeled
2 tablespoons Chinese
  Cabbage Kimchi

1 teaspoon salt
2 green onions, white
  parts only
1/2 cup (3 oz/90 g)
  ground pork
1 tablespoon crushed
  garlic paste
Oil, for frying

Dipping Sauce
3 tablespoons soy sauce
2 teaspoons vinegar
1 teaspoon sesame seed

Makes about 15 pancakes

3 Process the beans and water to a smooth paste in a blender. Add the sticky rice powder and mix well with a spoon.

1 Soak the beans in water overnight to soften.

2 Using your hands, gently rub the soaked beans together to remove the skins.

4 Mince the onion and kimchi. Sprinkle with the salt and set aside for about 15 minutes (do not rinse off the salt).

5 Cut the white parts of the green onion into thin strips.

6 Combine the pork, onion, kimchi and garlic in a bowl and mix well.

9 Heat 2 tablespoons of oil in a pan. Add 3 tablespoons of the batter into the hot oil and fry until golden brown, about 3 minutes on each side. Remove from the heat and drain on paper towels. Continue to fry the pancakes with the remaining ingredients in the same manner. Serve the pancakes whole or sliced, with the Dipping Sauce on the side.

7 Add the mung bean paste to the pork mixture and mix well.

8 To make the Dipping Sauce, combine the soy sauce and vinegar in a serving bowl and mix well. Set aside.

Mussels with Sweet Soy Dressing

1 lb (500 g) large mussels, scrubbed clean
2 oz (60 g) beef, sliced into very thin strips
1 tablespoon cornstarch, mixed with 1 tablespoon water

Soy Dressing
2 tablespoons soy sauce
1 cup (250 ml) water
1 tablespoon sugar
$^1/_2$ teaspoon freshly ground black pepper
1 teaspoon sesame oil

1 clove garlic, sliced
1 teaspoon grated fresh ginger root
1 green onion, white part only, cut into short lengths

1 Bring a large pot of lightly salted water to a boil. Add the mussels and simmer until the shells just open, 1–2 minutes. Remove from the heat and drain. Discard any shells that do not open. Remove and discard one of the shells from each mussel.
2 In a wok, bring the Soy Dressing ingredients to a boil over medium heat. Add the beef and simmer uncovered for 2–3 minutes. Reduce the heat to low, add the mussels and cornstarch mixture, and continue to simmer for 1–2 minutes, spooning the dressing over the mussels from time to time. Remove from the heat and serve hot.

Serves 4

Dried Fish Stew (Bugeojjim)

2 pieces dried pollack or cod, each 4 oz (125 g)
1 green onion, cut into short lengths
1 red chili pepper, sliced
1 tablespoon dry-roasted, ground pine nuts

Serves 4

Egg Strips
1 egg, white and yolk separated
Oil, for frying

Sauce
1/4 cup (60 ml) soy sauce
2 tablespoons sugar
4 teaspoons crushed garlic

2 teaspoons grated fresh ginger root
3 tablespoons minced green onions
4 teaspoons sesame paste
4 teaspoons sesame oil
1/2 teaspoon freshly ground black pepper
3 cups (750 ml) water

1 Pound the dried fish with a mallet or rolling pin to tenderize it, then cover with cold water and soak for 1 hour. Remove from the water and drain. Cut off the tail and fins of the fish, and remove and discard the spine along the entire length of the fish. Remove any other bones from the fish and cut it into bite-sized pieces.
2 Prepare the Egg Strips as described on page 47 and set aside.
3 Combine the Sauce ingredients in a bowl and mix well. Dip pieces of the fish, one by one, in the Sauce to coat them well. Transfer the coated fish to a saucepan and pour in the remaining Sauce. Cover and cook over medium heat until tender, about 30 minutes. Add the green onion, chili, Egg Strips and pine nuts and continue to simmer for 3–5 minutes. Remove from the heat and serve hot with steamed rice.

Tofu and Vegetable Soup

5 cups (1¹/₄ liters) water
One 4-in (10-cm) square piece dried kelp
1¹/₂ cups (40 g) dried anchovies
4 tablespoons soybean paste
4 teaspoons red chili paste
¹/₄ cup (50 g) beef strips
1 tablespoon minced garlic
1 cake (7 oz/200 g) firm tofu, diced
1 small zucchini, halved and sliced
1 red and 1 green chili peppers, diagonally sliced
Salt, to taste (optional)

1 Bring the water to a boil in a large saucepan. Add the kelp and anchovies, and return to a boil. Reduce the heat to medium-low and simmer uncovered for 15–20 minutes. Remove from the heat and strain. Reserve the clear stock, discard the kelp and anchovies.
2 Bring the stock to a boil over high heat. Add the soybean and red chili pastes and stir until they dissolve. Stir in all the other ingredients, except the chili, and return to a boil. Reduce the heat to medium-low and simmer uncovered for 3–5 minutes. Add the chili and adjust the taste with the salt as desired. Remove from the heat, ladle into individual serving bowls and serve hot with steamed rice.

Serves 4

Ginseng Chicken Soup (Samgyetang)

1 fresh chicken (about 2 lbs/1 kg)
8 cups (2 liters) water, or enough water to cover
1 green onion, minced
6 slices fresh ginger root
1 teaspoon salt, or to taste
¹/₂ teaspoon ground white pepper

Filling
¹/₃ cup (65 g) uncooked (glutinous) rice, washed, soaked for 30 minutes
6 cloves garlic, peeled
5 dried pitted red dates
2 flnger-thick ginseng roots, or 2 teaspoons ginseng powder

1 Clean the chicken, rinse well, then drain and pat dry with paper towels. In a bowl, combine the Filling ingredients and mix well, then spoon into the chicken's cavity. Sew up the opening with a needle and thread.
2 Place the chicken, water, green onion and ginger (and the ginseng powder if you are not using fresh roots) in a large pot. Cover tightly and bring to a boil over high heat. Reduce the heat to low and simmer for 1 hour. Skim off any fat from the surface of the soup and season with the salt and pepper before removing from the heat.
3 Remove the thread and spoon the Filling out into serving bowls. Using a knife, remove the chicken meat from the bones and divide equally among the serving bowls. Ladle the hot broth over and serve hot.

Serves 2–4

Mixed Seafood Stew

1 small daikon radish (5 oz/150 g), peeled and cubed

4 oz (125 g) fresh baby clams in shells, scrubbed and cleaned

3 oz (90 g) mussel meats (without shells)

4 fresh medium shrimp

1 fresh medium crab, scrubbed and cleaned, quartered

4 medium squid bodies, cut open and cleaned, or 1 small tenderized octopus, sliced

1 teaspoon salt, or to taste

$1/2$ cup (20 g) chrysanthemum leaves, cut into short lengths, or chopped celery

1 green onion, cut into short lengths

4 Korean watercress stems (*minari*), cut into short lengths

1 red chili pepper, deseeded and sliced

2 oz (60 g) enoki mushrooms, roots trimmed, separated

4 oz (125 g) dried udon noodles

Stock

8 cups (2 liters) water

1 cup (25 g) dried white bait or anchovies, rinsed

One 4-in (10-cm) square piece dried kelp

Seasoning

3 tablespoons Korean chili powder

1 tablespoon crushed garlic paste

2 teaspoons salt

1 tablespoon minced green onion

$1/2$ teaspoon freshly ground black pepper

$1/2$ teaspoon ginger juice (pressed from grated fresh ginger)

2 tablespoons rice wine

Serves 4

1 Prepare the Stock first by bringing the water to a boil in a stockpot. Add the dried white bait or anchovies and kelp, and return to a boil. Reduce the heat to low and simmer uncovered for about 30 minutes. Remove from the heat and strain. Reserve the clear Stock, discard the kelp and anchovies.

2 Combine the Seasoning ingredients in a small bowl and mix well, then pour into the Stock.

3 Place the radish in a pot and arrange the seafood on top of it in layers in the sequence as listed. Sprinkle with the salt, pour in the Stock and bring to a boil over high heat. Simmer uncovered for about 15 minutes, then stir in the chrysanthemum leaves or celery, green onion, watercress stems, chili and mushrooms. Return to a boil and continue to simmer for 2 more minutes, then add the udon noodles and cook for 5 minutes. Remove from the heat.

4 To serve, place the pot in the center of the dining table with serving bowls for your guests to help themselves.

Hearty Dumpling Soup

7 oz (200 g) beef
8 cups (2 liters) water
Sesame oil, to taste
Salt and freshly ground
  black pepper, to taste
30 Chinese wonton
  dumpling wrappers
1 tablespoon soy sauce,
  or to taste
1 green onion, sliced
  diagonally, to garnish

Filling
2 cups (100 g) bean
  sprouts, tails trimmed
1 cup (150 g) Chinese
  Cabbage Kimchi (page
  10), minced
5 oz (150 g) ground pork
$^1/_2$ cake (5 oz/ 150 g)
  soft tofu, drained and
  mashed with a fork
2 tablespoons minced
  green onion
1 tablespoon crushed
  garlic paste
1 teaspoon ginger juice
  (pressed from grated
  fresh ginger root)
1 teaspoon sesame paste
1 teaspoon salt
1 teaspoon ground white
  pepper
1 teaspoon sesame oil

Egg Strips
1 egg, white and yolk
  separated
Oil, for frying

1 In a saucepan, bring the beef and water to a boil
over high heat. Reduce the heat to low, simmer
uncovered for 30 minutes and remove from the heat.
Remove the beef from the stock and reserve the stock.
Thinly slice the beef and season with the sesame oil,
salt and pepper. Set aside.
2 Prepare the Filling by bringing a saucepan of water
to a boil and blanching the bean sprouts for 30 seconds.
Remove from the heat, drain well and roughly chop.
In a mixing bowl, combine the chopped bean sprouts
with all the other ingredients and mix well.
3 To make the dumplings, place $1^1/_2$ tablespoons of
the Filling in the center of a dumpling wrapper. Fold
the wrapper in half to form a semicircle, then wet the
edges with water and press them together to seal.
Continue to make the dumplings in the same manner
with the remaining ingredients.
4 Steam the dumplings in a steamer or covered wok
over rapidly boiling water for 6–7 minutes until
cooked. Remove from the heat and set aside.
5 Prepare the Egg Strips as described on page 47, but
slice it into diamond shapes. Set aside.
6 Bring the beef stock to a boil over high heat, season
with the soy sauce and simmer uncovered for 2–3
minutes. Add the green onion, beef slices and
steamed dumplings, and return to a boil. Remove
from the heat. Ladle into serving bowls, garnish with
the Egg Strips and serve hot.

Makes 30 dumplings or serves 6

Beef Ball Soup

4 oz (125 g) beef, thinly sliced
1 teaspoon crushed garlic paste
1 teaspoon sesame oil
1 teaspoon salt
Freshly ground black pepper, to taste
8 cups (2 liters) water
2 tablespoons soy sauce, or to taste

Meatballs
4 oz (125 g) ground beef
2 teaspoons minced green onion
1 cake (10 oz/300 g) soft tofu, crumbled
1 teaspoon crushed garlic
1 teaspoon sesame oil
1 teaspoon salt
Freshly ground black pepper, to taste

2 tablespoons oil
4 tablespoons flour
2 eggs, beaten

Egg Strips
1 egg, white and yolk separated
Oil, for frying

Serves 4–6

1 Prepare the Egg Strips as described on page 47 and set aside.
2 To make the Meatballs, combine the ground beef, green onion, tofu, garlic, sesame oil, salt and pepper in a bowl and mix until well blended. Wet your hands, spoon 1 tablespoon of the mixture and roll it into a ball. Continue to shape the Meatballs in the same manner with the remaining ingredients.
3 Heat the oil in a nonstick skillet over medium heat. Handling a few at a time, roll the Meatballs in the flour to coat well, then dip in the beaten egg and fry until evenly browned, about 2 minutes. Remove and drain on paper towels. Set aside.
4 In a saucepan, combine the beef slices, garlic, sesame oil, salt and pepper and mix until well coated. Add the water and bring to a boil over medium heat. Simmer uncovered for 20 minutes, then stir in the soy sauce. Reduce the heat to low, add the Meatballs and simmer uncovered for 5 minutes. Remove from the heat. Ladle the soup into individual serving bowls, top with the Egg Strips and serve hot.

Seaweed Soup with Clams or Mussels

1 cup (15 g) shredded dried seaweed
1 tablespoon sesame oil
1 tablespoon crushed garlic paste
1 cup (150 g) shelled clam or mussel meats
8 cups (2 liters) water
1$^1/_2$ tablespoons soy sauce, or to taste

1 Soak the seaweed in warm water for 20 minutes to allow it to expand. Rinse well in a couple of changes of water, then drain and squeeze dry.
2 Heat the oil in a pot over high heat and sauté the garlic and mussels or clams for 1 minute. Add the seaweed and sauté for 1 more minute. Pour in the water and bring the mixture to a boil. Reduce the heat to low and simmer uncovered for 15 minutes. Season with the soy sauce and remove from the heat. Ladle into individual serving bowls and serve hot.

Serves 4–6

Rice Bowl with Beef and Vegetables (Bibimbap)

7 oz (200 g) beef, sliced into thin strips
6 dried black Chinese mushrooms, soaked until soft, rinsed well and squeezed dry, stems trimmed, caps sliced
1 zucchini or Japanese cucumber, halved and thickly sliced diagonally
Pinch of salt
Oil, for frying and greasing
3 cups (150 g) bean sprouts, tails trimmed, blanched for 1 minute
5 oz (150 g) spinach, roots trimmed, chopped

4 cups (400 g) cooked rice
Nori seaweed strips, to garnish
Korean hot bean paste (*gochujang*), to serve
Sesame oil, to serve

Marinade
3 tablespoons soy sauce
4$^1/_2$ teaspoons sugar
2 tablespoons minced green onion
1 tablespoon crushed garlic paste
1 tablespoon sesame paste
1 tablespoon sesame oil

1 teaspoon freshly ground black pepper

Seasoning
2 teaspoons soy sauce
2 tablespoons minced green onion
1 tablespoon crushed garlic paste
$^1/_2$ teaspoon freshly ground black pepper

Egg Strips
2 eggs, white and yolk separated

Serves 4

1 Combine the Marinade ingredients in a bowl and mix well, then divide into 2 equal portions. Marinate the beef and mushroom, separately, in the Marinade for about 20 minutes. Sprinkle the zucchini or cucumber slices with a pinch of salt and set aside for 10 minutes, then squeeze out any excess moisture.
2 Heat 1 tablespoon of the oil in a nonstick skillet over medium heat and sauté the marinated mushroom for 2–3 minutes. Remove from the heat. In the same pan, heat another tablespoon of the oil and sauté the beef strips for 2–3 minutes until evenly browned, followed by the zucchini or cucumber slices for 1–2 minutes. Remove from the heat and drain on paper towels.
3 Combine the Seasoning ingredients in a bowl and mix well. Pour $^1/_2$ of the Seasoning over the blanched bean sprouts and toss until well coated.

4 Heat 1 tablespoon of the oil in a skillet over high heat and sauté the spinach for about 2 minutes until wilted, seasoning with the remaining Seasoning. Remove from the heat.

5 To make the Egg Strips, lightly grease a clean nonstick skillet and heat over medium heat until hot. Pour in the egg white, tilting the pan to form a thin layer. Reduce the heat to low and cook until set, 1–2 minutes. Remove from the heat and set aside to cool. Repeat to fry the egg yolks in the same manner. Thinly slice the cooked egg.

6 Divide the rice among 4 serving bowls and top each with equal amounts of the beef, mushroom, zucchini or cucumber, bean sprouts, spinach and Egg Strips. Garnish with the nori strips and serve with bowls of Korean hot bean paste and sesame oil on the side.

Mixed Beef, Vegetable and Egg Bibimbap

1 red radish (about 2 oz/60 g), peeled and cut into matchsticks
1 small daikon radish (about 4 oz/125 g), peeled and cut into matchsticks
1 carrot, peeled and cut into matchsticks
1 small cucumber, peeled and cut into matchsticks
4 shiso leaves, cut into thin strips (optional)

5 lettuce leaves, cut into thin strips
7 oz (200 g) beef, cut into thin strips
3 tablespoons oil
4 eggs
4 cups (400 g) cooked rice

Marinade
1 tablespoon soy sauce
1 1/2 teaspoons sugar
2 teaspoons minced green onion
1 teaspoon crushed garlic paste

1 teaspoon sesame paste
1 teaspoon sesame oil
Pinch of freshly ground black pepper

Hot Bean Paste Dressing
2 tablespoons Korean hot bean paste (*gochujang*)
3 tablespoons beef stock or water
2 tablespoons sugar
1 tablespoon sesame oil
2 teaspoons sesame paste

Serves 4

1 Keep all the vegetables fresh by soaking them, separately, in iced water and then drain well.
2 Combine the Marinade ingredients in a bowl and mix well. Add the beef strips and mix until well coated. Allow to marinate for 10 minutes. Heat 1 tablespoon of the oil in a nonstick skillet over high heat and sauté the marinated beef until browned and cooked, 2–3 minutes. Removed from the heat and set aside.
3 Clean the skillet and heat the remaining oil over medium-low heat until hot and fry each egg, sunny-side up, until set. Remove from the heat and set aside.
4 Prepare the Hot Bean Paste Dressing by combining all the ingredients in a serving bowl and mix well.
5 Divide the rice among 4 serving bowls, top with equal amounts of the beef, vegetables and a fried egg and serve with the bowl of Hot Bean Paste Dressing on the side. Invite your guests to add a little dressing to the bowl, then mix the rice, egg, meat and vegetables thoroughly before eating.

You can use any vegetables you like. Seasonal vegetables are the best. Traditionally, the ingredients are arranged over the rice in grouped vertical segments, and topped with an egg.

Noodles with Beef and Sesame (Japchae)

5 oz (150 g) beef, cut into thin strips
4 dried black Chinese mushrooms, soaked until soft, rinsed well and squeezed dry, stems trimmed, caps sliced
8 oz (250 g) *dangmyeon* or dried glass noodles
1 tablespoon oil
3 cloves garlic, minced

1 carrot, peeled and cut into matchsticks
1 onion, thinly sliced
$1/_2$ teaspoon salt
$1/_2$ teaspoon ground white pepper

Marinade
2 tablespoons soy sauce
1 tablespoon sugar
1 green onion, minced
1 tablespoon sesame oil

Seasoned Spinach
5 oz (150 g) spinach, roots trimmed, sliced
1 teaspoon sesame paste
$1/_2$ teaspoon salt
Pinch of freshly ground black pepper

Egg Strips
1 egg, white and yolk separated
Oil, for frying

1 Combine the Marinade ingredients in a large bowl and mix well. Add the beef and mushroom and mix until well coated. Allow to marinate for 20 minutes.
2 To make the Seasoned Spinach, bring a saucepan of water to a boil and blanch the spinach for 1-2 minutes. Remove from the heat, rinse in cold water and drain. Squeeze out any excess water from the spinach. Place the spinach in a bowl and season with the sesame paste, salt and pepper. Set aside.
3 Bring the saucepan of water to a boil again and cook the noodles until soft, 2–3 minutes. Remove from the heat, rinse the noodles in cold water and drain well.
4 Prepare the Egg Strips as described on page 47 and set aside.
5 Heat the oil in a nonstick wok over high heat and stir-fry the garlic until fragrant and golden brown, about 30 seconds. Add the marinated beef and mushroom and the Marinade, and stir-fry until cooked, 1–2 minutes. Add the vegetables and stir-fry for 2–3 minutes, seasoning with the salt and pepper. Stir in the noodles and toss until well blended, adjusting the taste with more seasonings as desired. Remove from the heat. Transfer to serving platters, top with the Egg Strips and serve hot.

Serves 4

Beef Noodle Soup (Onmyeon)

10 oz (300 g) beef
12 cups (3 liters) water
1 green onion
3 cloves garlic, peeled
2 tablespoons soy sauce
1 teaspoon salt, or to
  taste
1 zucchini or Japanese
  cucumber, cut into thin
  strips
Pinch of salt
1 tablespoon oil
4 dried black Chinese
  mushrooms, soaked
  until soft, rinsed well
  and squeezed dry, stems
  trimmed, caps sliced
10 oz (300 g) dried ramen
  or wheat noodles
  (*somyeon*)

Egg Strips
2 eggs, white and yolk
  separated
Oil, for frying

Serves 4

1 In a pot, bring the beef, water, green onion and garlic to a boil over high heat. Reduce the heat to low and simmer uncovered until the beef is tender and the stock has reduced to two-thirds, 30–45 minutes. Remove from the heat.

2 Remove the beef from the broth and slice thinly. Skim any fat from the surface, then season the broth with the soy sauce and salt. Keep the broth simmering over very low heat.

3 Prepare the Egg Strips as described on page 47 and set aside.

4 Sprinkle the zucchini or cucumber with a pinch of salt and set aside for 10 minutes. Squeeze out any excess water from the zucchini or cucumber. Set aside.

5 Heat the oil in a skillet over high heat and sauté the mushroom until fragrant and browned, 1–2 minutes. Remove from the heat and set aside.

6 Bring a saucepan of water to a boil and blanch the noodles, stirring to prevent the noodles from sticking together, until soft, 3–5 minutes. Remove from the heat, rinse in cold water and drain well. Divide equally among 4 serving bowls.

7 Top the noodles in each bowl with equal amounts of the beef, vegetables and Egg Strips. Ladle the hot broth over and serve hot.

Cold Buckwheat Noodles (Naengmyeon)

10 oz (300 g) beef
12 cups (3 liters) water
1 green onion
3 cloves garlic, peeled
1 zucchini or Japanese cucumber, halved and thinly sliced
Pinch of salt
1 lb (500 g) dried buckwheat (*naengmyeon*) or soba noodles
1 pear (preferably nashi), peeled, cored and thinly sliced
Few tablespoons sliced cabbage or radish kimchi
2 hardboiled eggs, halved
Hot prepared mustard, sugar and vinegar, to serve

Seasoning
1 teaspoon salt, or to taste
2 tablespoons sugar
2 tablespoons vinegar
2 tablespoons soy sauce

1 In a pot, bring the beef, water, green onion and garlic to a boil over high heat, skimming off any fat and froth that float to the surface. Reduce the heat to low and simmer uncovered until the beef is tender and the stock has reduced to two-thirds, 30–45 minutes. Remove from the heat.

2 Remove the beef from the stock and slice thinly. Add the Seasoning to the stock, adjusting according to taste. Set aside to cool, then chill the broth in the refrigerator for 30 minutes.

3 Sprinkle the zucchini or cucumber with a pinch of salt and set aside for 10 minutes. Squeeze out any excess water from the zucchini or cucumber.

4 Bring a saucepan of water to a boil and cook the noodles, stirring to prevent the noodles from sticking together, until soft, about 5 minutes. Remove from the heat, rinse in cold water and drain well. Divide equally among 4 serving bowls.

5 Top the noodles in each bowl with equal amounts of the beef, zucchini or cucumber, pear, kimchi and an egg half. Ladle the chilled broth over and serve with mustard, sugar and vinegar on the side.

Serves 4

Noodle Bowl with Beef and Vegetables (Bibimmyeon)

3 dried black Chinese mushrooms, soaked until soft, rinsed well and squeezed dry, stems trimmed, caps sliced
5 oz (150 g) beef, sliced into thin strips
1 zucchini or Japanese cucumber, halved and thinly sliced diagonally
Pinch of salt
Oil, for frying
10 oz (300 g) dried ramen or wheat noodles (somyeon)

1 red chili pepper, deseeded, sliced into thin strips, to garnish

Marinade
1 tablespoon soy sauce
1 1/2 teaspoons sugar
2 teaspoons minced green onion
1 teaspoon crushed garlic paste
1 teaspoon sesame paste
1 teaspoon sesame oil
Freshly round black pepper, to taste

Egg Strips
2 eggs, white and yolk separated

Chili Pepper Sauce
2 tablespoons Korean hot bean paste (gochujang)
3 tablespoons soy sauce
2 tablespoons sugar
1 tablespoon sesame oil
1 1/2 teaspoons sesame paste

Serves 4

1 Combine the Marinade ingredients in a large bowl and mix well. Add the mushroom and beef strips, and mix until well coated. Allow to marinate for 30 minutes.
2 Sprinkle the zucchini or cucumber with the salt and set aside for 10 minutes. Squeeze out any excess water from the zucchini or cucumber. Set aside.
3 Heat 1 tablespoon of oil in a nonstick skillet over high heat until hot and sauté the marinated beef and mushroom until browned on all sides, 2–3 minutes. Remove from the heat and set aside. Clean the pan and sauté the zucchini or cucumber slices in 1 teaspoon of oil for 1–2 minutes. Remove from the heat and set aside.
4 Prepare the Egg Strips as described on page 47 and set aside.
5 Bring a saucepan of water to a boil and blanch the noodles, stirring to prevent the noodles from sticking together, until soft, 3–5 minutes. Remove from the heat, rinse in cold water and drain well. Transfer the noodles to a large bowl and add the sautéed beef and mushroom, and 1/2 of the zucchini or cucumber slices.
6 Combine the Chili Pepper Sauce ingredients in a small bowl and mix well. Pour the sauce over the noodles and toss until well blended. Divide the noodles equally among 4 serving platters. Top with the Egg Strips and remaining zucchini or cucumber slices, and serve hot, garnished with the chili strips.

Abalone Porridge (Jeonbokjuk)

1 cup (200 g) uncooked rice, washed, soaked in water for 30 minutes, then drained
6 cups (1 1/2 liters) water
1 tablespoon sesame oil
1 large or 2 small canned abalones, drained, thinly sliced
1 teaspoon salt, or to taste

1 Process the rice and 1 cup (250 ml) of the water to a coarse paste in a blender.
2 Heat the sesame oil in a nonstick wok over medium heat. Add the abalone and processed rice, and cook for 10 minutes, stirring. Add the remaining water and bring to a boil. Reduce the heat to low and simmer uncovered until most of the liquid has been absorbed, 20–30 minutes. Remove from the heat. Season with the salt just before serving.

Serves 4

Soybean Porridge (Kongjuk)

1/2 cup (100 g) dried soybeans, soaked in water for 5–6 hours, then drained
Water
1 cup (200 g) uncooked rice, washed, soaked in water for 30 minutes, then drained
Salt, to taste (optional)

Serves 4

1 Bring the soybeans and water (enough to cover) to a boil in a saucepan. Remove from the heat, drain and rinse the soybeans in cold water. When cool enough to handle, rub the soybeans together with your hands to remove the transparent husks (they will float to the surface). Pour out the water and husks. Repeat the boiling and rubbing processes until all the husks are removed from the soybeans.
2 Process the soybeans and 1 cup (250 ml) of water to a paste in a blender. Set aside.
3 In a saucepan, bring the rice and 2 cups (500 ml) of water to a boil over high heat, then simmer uncovered for 5 minutes. Remove from the heat, rinse the rice in cold water and drain. Process the boiled rice with 1 cup (250 ml) of water to a smooth paste in a blender.
4 In a large saucepan, bring the processed soybean to a boil and simmer uncovered for 3–5 minutes. Add the processed rice and 4 cups (1 liter) of water, and return to a boil. Reduce the heat to a simmer, cook uncovered for a further 20 minutes and remove from the heat. Ladle into serving bowls and serve, sprinkled with salt (if using).

Pine Nut Porridge (Jatjuk)

$^1/_2$ cup (50 g) pine nuts
5 cups (1$^1/_4$ liters) water
1 cup (200 g) uncooked
  rice, washed and soaked
  for 30 minutes, then
  drained
Salt, to serve (optional)

Serves 4–6

1 Process the pine nuts and 1 cup (250 ml) of the water in a blender until smooth. Set aside.
2 Clean the blender and process the rice and 1 cup (250 ml) of the water to a coarse paste. Transfer to a nonstick saucepan, add the remaining water and cook, stirring occasionally, over medium heat for 15 minutes. Reduce the heat to low, stir in the processed pine nut and simmer uncovered for a further 15 minutes. Remove from the heat, ladle into serving bowls and serve with a serving bowl of salt (if using) on the side.

Mung Bean Porridge (Nokdujuk)

1 cup (200 g) dried
  mung beans, soaked for
  2 hours, then drained
12 cups (3 liters) water
1 cup (200 g) uncooked
  rice, washed and soaked
  for 30 minutes, then
  drained
Salt, to serve (optional)

Serves 6

1 In a large saucepan, bring the mung beans and 8 cups (2 liters) of the water to a boil over high heat. Simmer uncovered until the beans are soft, 20–30 minutes. Remove from the heat and drain, reserving the bean water. Process the cooked mung beans to a paste in a blender, adding the bean water gradually. Set aside.
2 In a large saucepan, bring the soaked rice and remaining water to a boil over medium heat, stirring occasionally. Add the mung bean paste and return to a boil. Reduce the heat to low and simmer uncovered, until the rice turns soggy, about 20 minutes. Remove from the heat, ladle into serving bowls and serve with a serving bowl of salt (if using) on the side.

Soy Ginger Chicken (Dakjjim)

1 fresh chicken (about
  3 lbs/1$^1/_3$ kg), cleaned
  and dried, cut into bite-
  sized pieces
1 large potato, peeled
  and cubed
1 large carrot, peeled and
  cubed
3 onions, cut into wedges
1 green onion, cut into
  short lengths

Seasoning
$^1/_2$ cup (125 ml) soy
  sauce
3 tablespoons sugar
3 tablespoons minced
  green onions
2 tablespoons crushed
  garlic paste
2 tablespoons ginger
  juice (pressed from
  grated fresh ginger root)
2 tablespoons rice wine
$^1/_2$ teaspoon salt
$^1/_2$ teaspoon freshly
  ground black pepper
1 teaspoon sesame oil

Egg Strips
1 egg, white and yolk
  separated
Oil, for frying

1 Combine the Seasoning ingredients in a bowl and mix well. Set aside for 10 minutes to allow the flavors to blend.

2 Prepare the Egg Strips as described on page 47 and set aside.

3 Place the chicken pieces in a pot and add enough of water to cover. Bring the mixture to a boil, then simmer uncovered over medium-low heat, skimming off any fat and froth that float to the surface. Pour in half of the Seasoning and continue simmering for 15 minutes. Add the vegetables and remaining Seasoning, and cook until the vegetables are tender but not mushy, about 15 minutes. Remove from the heat. Garnish with the Egg Strips and serve hot with steamed rice.

Serves 6

Grilled Chicken Drumsticks

4 chicken drumsticks
1 tablespoon ginger juice (pressed from grated fresh
  ginger root)
2 tablespoons oil
2 tablespoons soy sauce
1 tablespoon sugar
1 tablespoon malt liquid
1 tablespoon rice wine
Chopped parsley, to garnish

1 Rinse the chicken well, then dry with paper towels.
Score each drumstick with the tip of a sharp knife at
several spots. Place the drumsticks in a bowl, pour the
ginger juice over and rub the juice into them. Leave
the drumsticks to marinate for 15 minutes, turning
frequently to coat with the ginger juice.
2 Heat the oil in a wok over medium heat until hot.
Fry the marinated drumsticks until golden, about
5 minutes. Remove from the heat and drain on
paper towels.
3 Combine the soy sauce, sugar, malt and rice wine in
a small bowl. Pour the mixture into the wok with the
leftover oil and bring to a boil over high heat. Reduce
the heat to low and simmer uncovered until the sauce
has reduced to half, about 5 minutes. Remove from
the heat.
4 Using a brush, coat each drumstick with the sauce.
Return the drumsticks and the sauce to the wok and
cook over low heat until the sauce caramelizes and
the chicken is cooked through, about 5 minutes.
Remove from the heat and serve hot, garnished with
the parsley.

Serves 4

Grilled Chicken Wings

6 chicken wings
Pinch of sesame salt
1 tablespoon ginger juice
   (pressed from grated
   fresh ginger root)
4 tablespoons cornstarch
Oil, for deep-frying

Sesame oil, to taste

Sweet Sauce
2 tablespoons soy sauce
1 tablespoon malt liquid
1 tablespoon sugar
1 teaspoon ginger juice

1 tablespoon rice wine
3 tablespoons water
5 cloves garlic, minced
2 red chili peppers,
   halved and deseeded

Serves 4

1 Rinse the chicken wings and pat dry with paper towels. Place the chicken wings in a large bowl, add the sesame salt and ginger juice and mix well, then coat the chicken wings with the cornstarch.

2 Heat the oil in a wok or deep-frier over medium heat until hot and deep-fry the wings until golden, 5–10 minutes. Remove from the pan and drain on paper towels.

3 To make the Sweet Sauce, bring the soy sauce, malt liquid, sugar, ginger juice, rice wine and water to a boil over medium heat in a large saucepan. Stir in the garlic and chili and simmer uncovered, stirring occasionally, until the sauce is reduced to half, 3–5 minutes. Remove from the heat.

4 Add the deep-fried chicken wings to the Sweet Sauce and mix until the wings are well coated with the sauce. Sprinkle the wings with sesame oil and serve with steamed rice.

Marinated Chicken Breast (Dakgaseum Gui)

4 boneless chicken
   breasts, sliced into bite-
   sized pieces
2 tablespoons oil
Lettuce leaves, to serve

Serves 4

Marinade
3 tablespoons soy sauce
2 tablespoons sugar
2 tablespoons rice wine
1 teaspoon ginger juice
   (pressed from grated
   fresh ginger root)

1 tablespoon crushed
   garlic paste
1 green onion, minced
1 teaspoon sesame salt
Pinch of freshly ground
   black pepper
1 teaspoon sesame oil

1 Combine the Marinade ingredients in a large bowl and mix well. Add the chicken pieces and mix until well coated. Cover and marinate in the refrigerator for at least 3 hours.

2 Heat the oil in a wok over medium heat until hot. Stir-fry the chicken with the Marinade until cooked, 3–5 minutes. Remove from the heat.

3 Arrange the lettuce leaves on a serving platter and top with the chicken pieces. Serve hot with steamed rice.

Ginger Pork

10 oz (300 g) pork tenderloin, cut into bite-sized pieces
$^1/_2$ cup (60 g) cornstarch
Oil, for deep-frying
3 cloves garlic, sliced
1 red chili pepper, deseeded, cut into thin strips
3 green onions, cut into short lengths
2 tablespoons soy sauce
2 tablespoons malt liquid
Freshly ground black pepper, to taste
Sesame oil, to taste
Lettuce leaves, to serve

Marinade
1 teaspoon salt
1 tablespoon ginger juice (pressed from grated fresh
   ginger root)
2 tablespoons rice wine

1 Combine the Marinade ingredients in a large bowl
and mix well. Add the pork pieces and mix until well
coated. Cover and marinate in the refrigerator for
2–3 hours.
2 Heat the oil in a wok over high heat. Roll the marinated pork pieces in the cornstarch to coat well, then
deep-fry in the hot oil for about 1 minute. Remove
from the heat and drain on paper towels.
3 Heat 1 tablespoon of the oil in a clean wok over
medium heat and stir-fry the garlic and chili for
1–2 minutes until fragrant and golden brown. Add
the pork and continue to stir-fry for 2–3 minutes.
Add the green onion and stir-fry for 1 minute, seasoning with the soy sauce, malt and pepper. Sprinkle with
a few drops of sesame oil and remove from the heat.
4 Arrange the lettuce leaves on a serving platter and
top with the stir-fried pork. Serve the dish hot with
steamed rice.

Serves 4

Glazed Beef Ribs (Galbijjim)

1½ lbs (750 g) beef ribs, chopped into bite-sized pieces
4 cups (1 liter) water
1 small daikon radish (5 oz/150 g), peeled and cubed, blanched for 1 minute
1 carrot, peeled and cubed, blanched for 1 minute

8 dried black Chinese mushrooms, soaked until soft, rinsed well and squeezed dry, stems trimmed (optional)

Egg Strips
1 egg, white and yolk separated
Oil, for frying

Seasoning
3 tablespoons soy sauce
3 tablespoons pear juice or grated pear
1 tablespoon sugar
2 green onions, minced
2 cloves garlic, crushed
1 tablespoon sesame oil
1 teaspoon sesame paste
2 tablespoons malt liquid
½ teaspoon freshly ground black pepper

1 Soak the beef pieces in a large bowl of water for 1 hour, then rinse well and drain. In a large saucepan, bring the beef pieces and water to a boil over medium heat and simmer uncovered, skimming off any fat and froth that float to the surface, until the stock reduces to half, 15–20 minutes. Remove from the heat.
2 Prepare the Egg Strips as described on page 47, but slice it into diamond shapes. Set aside.
3 Combine the Seasoning ingredients in a bowl and mix well.
4 Remove the beef pieces from the stock. Add the Seasoning to the beef stock and simmer over low heat for 5 minutes. Increase the heat to medium, stir in the beef and all the vegetables, and continue cooking for about 10 minutes, until the beef is tender. Remove from the heat. Garnish with the Egg Strips and serve hot with steamed rice.

Serves 4

Marinated Grilled Beef

$1/_2$ cup (125 ml) pear juice or $1/_2$ cup (100 g) grated
  pear (preferably nashi)
3 tablespoons rice wine
1 lb (500 g) beef tenderloin, sliced into strips
Shiso leaves or lettuce leaves, to serve
1 green onion, sliced into thin strips, soaked in iced
  water and drained
1 red chili pepper, deseeded and sliced into thin strips
Few drops of sesame oil (optional)

Marinade
1 teaspoon salt
$1^1/_2$ tablespoons sugar
$1^1/_2$ tablespoons minced green onion
1 tablespoon crushed garlic paste
1 teaspoon sesame paste
$1/_2$ teaspoon freshly ground black pepper, to taste
2 teaspoons sesame oil

1 Combine the pear juice or grated pear and rice wine
in a bowl. Add the beef slices and mix well. Set aside
for 30 minutes, then drain.
2 In a bowl, combine the Marinade ingredients and
mix until the sugar is dissolved. Pour the Marinade
over the beef strips and mix until well coated. Cover
and marinate in the refrigerator for 2–3 hours.
3 Preheat a pan grill or broiler over medium heat
until hot. Grill the marinated beef strips in several
batches, basting with the Marinade, until the desired
tenderness, 2–3 minutes on each side.
4 Arrange the shiso or lettuce leaves on a serving
platter and top with the grilled beef strips. Sprinkle
the beef with a few drops of sesame oil (to give it a
sheen), garnish with the green onion and chili strips,
and serve hot with steamed rice.

Serves 4

Grilled Beef Kebabs

7 oz (200 g) beef, cubed
1 green onion, cut into
  short lengths
1 green bell pepper,
  deseeded, thickly sliced
4–8 bamboo skewers,
  soaked in water for 1
  hour before using
Oil, for frying
Lettuce leaves, to serve

Marinade
2 tablespoons soy sauce
2 teaspoons sugar
1 tablespoon minced
  green onion
1 teaspoon sesame paste
1 teaspoon sesame oil

1 In a large bowl, combine the Marinade ingredients and mix until the sugar is dissolved. Add the beef and mix until well coated. Allow to marinate for 15–20 minutes.
2 Thread the marinated beef cubes, alternating with the green onion and bell pepper slices, onto the bamboo skewers. Brush each skewer with the Marinade, coating both sides well.
3 Heat a little oil in a nonstick skillet over high heat until hot and fry the skewers for about 2 minutes on each side. Alternatively, grill the skewers in a pan grill or oven. Arrange the lettuce leaves on serving platters and top with the kebabs. Serve immediately with steamed rice.

Serves 4

Marinated Grilled Pork

1 lb (500 g) pork tender-
  loin, sliced into strips

Marinade
1 1/2 tablespoons Korean
  hot bean paste (gochu-
  jang)

2 tablespoons soy sauce
2 teaspoons sesame oil
1 teaspoon sesame paste
1 1/2 tablespoons minced
  green onion
1 tablespoon crushed
  garlic paste

1 1/2 teaspoons grated
  fresh ginger root
1/2 onion, minced
Freshly ground black
  pepper, to taste

Serves 4

1 In a large bowl, combine the Marinade ingredients and mix well. Add the pork strips and mix until well coated. Cover and marinate in the refrigerator for 2–3 hours.
2 Preheat a pan grill or broiler over medium heat until hot. Grill the marinated pork strips in several batches, basting with the Marinade, until cooked, 2–3 minutes on each side. Remove from the heat and serve immediately with steamed rice.

Pork with Kimchi and Tofu

Oil, for frying
7 oz (200 g) Chinese Cabbage Kimchi (page 10), sliced
$^1/_2$ onion, sliced
7 oz (200 g) pork belly, thinly sliced
1 tablespoon crushed garlic paste
2 tablespoons minced green onion
1 tablespoon sesame oil
1 teaspoon sesame paste.
1 cake (10 oz/300 g) firm tofu

1 Heat 1 tablespoon of oil in a wok over medium heat and stir-fry the kimchi, onion, pork, garlic and green onion fro 3–5 minutes until the pork is well cooked. Remove from the heat, add the sesame oil and sesame paste to the pan and mix well.
2 Bring a saucepan of water to a boil and blanch the tofu for 10 seconds. Remove from the heat and drain. Slice the tofu into $1^1/_2$ x $^3/_4$-in (4 x 2-cm) pieces.
3 To serve, place the stir-fried pork in the center of a serving platter and arrange the tofu pieces around it. Serve hot with steamed rice.

Serves 4

Ground Beef Squares with Tofu and Sesame

5 oz (150 g) firm tofu
7 oz (200 g) ground beef
2 tablespoons soy sauce
1 teaspoon salt
1 tablespoon sugar
2 tablespoons minced green onion
1 tablespoon crushed garlic paste
2 teaspoons sesame paste
1 tablespoon sesame oil
1 tablespoon dry-roasted, ground pine nuts

1 Wrap the tofu in a clean cloth and gently squeeze out the excess water. In a bowl, mash the tofu with a fork. Add the beef, soy sauce, salt, sugar, green onion, garlic, sesame paste and sesame oil, and mix until well blended.
2 Divide the beef and tofu mixture into 2 equal portions and form each portion into a patty. Place each patty on a greased aluminum foil sheet.
3 Place the aluminum sheet with the patty on a pre-heated pan grill or under a broiler and grill to desired doneness, 5–7 minutes on each side. Remove from the heat and set aside to cool. Slice each patty into rectangular pieces. Arrange on a serving platter, sprinkle with the ground pine nut and serve.

Serves 4–6

Black Pepper Beef Kebabs

8 oz (250 g) ground beef
1 tablespoon crushed garlic paste
1 teaspoon freshly ground black pepper
2 teaspoons sesame oil
Oil, for greasing and frying
4 gingko nuts, cracked to obtain fruits, peeled
20 pine nuts
1 teaspoon malt liquid
4 bamboo skewers

Sauce
2 tablespoons soy sauce
2 teaspoons sugar
2 teaspoons rice wine
3 tablespoons water

1 In a large bowl, combine the beef, garlic, pepper and 1 teaspoon of the sesame oil and mix until well blended. Divide the beef mixture into 4 equal portions and shape each portion into a patty. Place the patties on a greased aluminum foil sheet and cook in a skillet over medium heat for 2–3 minutes on each side. Remove from the heat.
2 Bring the Sauce ingredients to a boil in a saucepan, then simmer uncovered over low heat, stirring, for 2–3 minutes. Add the beef patties and cook until browned, about 10 minutes. Remove from the heat and stir in the remaining sesame oil.
3 Heat a little oil in a skillet over medium heat and fry the gingko nuts until they become transparent. Remove from heat. Brush the pine nuts with the malt liquid and set aside.
4 To serve, thread each beef patty horizontally onto a skewer, followed by 1 gingko nut. Stud each patty with 5 pine nuts.

Serves 4

Beef with Mushrooms and Bamboo Shoots

1 fresh or 10-oz (300-g) can bamboo shoot
5 cups (1¼ liters) rice water (reserved after washing rice)
1 dried red chili
Oil, for frying
6 Korean watercress stems (*minari*), cut into short lengths
3 dried black Chinese mushrooms, soaked until soft, rinsed well and squeezed dry, stems trimmed, caps sliced

5 oz (150 g) beef, sliced into 1-in (3-cm) strips
1 cup (100 g) bean sprouts, tails trimmed, blanched for 1 minute
1 red chili pepper, deseeded, cut into thin strips

Marinade
2 tablespoons soy sauce
1 tablespoon sugar
1½ tablespoons minced green onion
2 teaspoons crushed garlic paste

2 teaspoons sesame oil
1 teaspoon sesame paste
Freshly ground black pepper, to taste

Egg Strips
1 egg, white and yolk separated

Dressing
1 tablespoon soy sauce
1 teaspoon salt
2 teaspoons sugar
1 tablespoon vinegar
1 teaspoon sesame paste

1 If using fresh bamboo shoot, bring the rice water to a boil over medium heat in a large saucepan and simmer the bamboo shoot with the dried chili for 1 hour. Remove from the heat and set aside to cool, then peel the blanched bamboo shoot. Omit this step if using the canned bamboo shoot. Slice the cooked or canned bamboo shoot into 2 in (5 cm) long slices.

2 Heat 1 tablespoon of oil in a skillet and sauté the bamboo shoot slices over medium heat for 2–3 minutes. Remove from the heat. In the same pan, sauté the watercress stem in 1 teaspoon of oil for 2–3 minutes.

3 Combine the Marinade ingredients in a large bowl and mix well. Add the beef and mushroom and mix until well coated. Allow to marinate for 15 minutes. Heat 1 tablespoon of oil in a nonstick skillet and sauté the marinated beef and mushrooms over high heat until browned, 2–3 minutes. Remove from the heat and set aside.

4 Prepare the Egg Strips as described on page 47 and set aside.

5 Combine the bamboo shoot slices, watercress stem, beef and mushroom, bean sprouts and chili in a mixing bowl. In a small bowl, combine all the Dressing ingredients and mix until the sugar is dissolved. Pour the Dressing over the ingredients in the mixing bowl and toss thoroughly. Transfer to a serving platter, top with the Egg Strips and serve immediately with steamed rice.

Serves 4–6

Squid Bulgogi

4–5 medium squid bodies (about 10 oz/300 g in total), cut open and cleaned
4 dried black Chinese mushrooms, soaked until soft, rinsed well and squeezed dry, stems trimmed, caps roughly chopped
2 small green bell peppers, cored and deseeded, cut into bite-sized pieces
2 tablespoons oil
Lettuce leaves, to serve
1 teaspoon dry-roasted sesame seeds
Freshly ground black pepper, to taste
1 tablespoon thin red chili pepper strips (optional)

Marinade
3 tablespoons soy sauce
2 tablespoons sugar
2 tablespoons crushed garlic paste
2 tablespoons minced green onion
1 teaspoon ginger juice (pressed from grated fresh ginger root)
1 teaspoon sesame oil

1 Using the tip of a knife, score the surface of the squid in a crisscross pattern to prevent it from over curling during cooking. Slice the squid into bite-sized pieces.
2 Combine the Marinade ingredients in a large bowl and mix well. Add the squid pieces, mushroom and bell pepper pieces, and mix until well coated. Allow to marinate for 20–30 minutes, then drain.
3 Heat the oil in a wok over high heat until very hot and stir-fry the marinated ingredients until cooked, 2–3 minutes. Remove from the heat.
4 Arrange the lettuce leaves on individual serving platters and top with the Squid Bulgogi. Sprinkle with the sesame seeds, black pepper and chili strips (if using), and serve with steamed rice.

Serves 4

Red Pepper Grilled Fish

2 fresh flounder or sole, about 10 oz (300 g) each
1 teaspoon sesame oil
1 tablespoon soy sauce
6 tablespoons oil

Red Chili Sauce
2 tablespoons Korean hot bean paste (*gochujang*)
2 tablespoons minced green onion
1 tablespoon crushed garlic paste
1 1/2 tablespoons crushed ginger
1 tablespoon sesame oil
2 teaspoons sesame paste
Pinch of freshly ground black or white pepper

Serves 4

1 Scale, gut and clean the fish, then make several shallow diagonal cuts on each side. Pat the fish dry with paper towels. Combine the sesame oil and soy sauce and mix well, then rub the mixture into the fish and set aside for 10 minutes.

2 Combine the Red Chili Sauce ingredients in a small bowl and mix well.

3 Heat 3 tablespoons of the oil in a wok over high heat until very hot. Gently lower the fish into the hot oil and fry until golden, 2–3 minutes. Turn the fish over and fry the other side for a further 3 minutes. Reduce the heat to low, add half of the Red Chili Sauce to the fish, turning the fish to coat well. Continue to fry the fish, turning once or twice, until the sauce darkens and almost dries up, 2–3 minutes. Remove from the heat. Repeat to fry the remaining fish in the same manner. Serve immediately with steamed rice.

4 Alternatively, fry the fish until cooked and crisp, remove from the heat and brush with the Red Chili Sauce on both sides.

For a variation, you can substitute the Red Chili Sauce for a non spicy version: 1/3 cup (90 ml) soy sauce, 1 1/2 tablespoons grated fresh ginger root, 1 tablespoon sugar, 1 tablespoon crushed garlic paste, 2 tablespoons minced green onion, 1 teaspoon sesame paste, 1 1/2 teaspoons sesame oil and a pinch of freshly ground black pepper.

Grilled Seafood Kebabs

1 small fresh octopus (about 1 lb/500 g)
1 tablespoon salt
2–3 medium squid bodies (about 7 oz/200 g in total), cut open and cleaned
10 oz (300 g) fish fillets, sliced into bite-sized pieces
2 green bell peppers, cored and deseeded, then cut into pieces
6 oz (180 g) oyster mushrooms, blanched, sliced into pieces
30 bamboo skewers, soaked in water for 1 hour before using
Oil, for frying or grilling

Chili Paste Sauce
4 tablespoons Korean hot bean paste (*gochujang*)
2 tablespoons crushed garlic paste
3 tablespoons minced green onions
1 teaspoon ginger juice (pressed from grated fresh ginger root)
2 tablespoons sugar
2 teaspoons sesame paste
2 teaspoons sesame oil

Serves 6

1 Clean the octopus by removing the eyes, mouth area, viscera and ink sac (or have your seafood supplier do this for you). Rinse the octopus well, rub thoroughly with the salt, then rinse again. Bring a large saucepan of water to a boil, immerse the octopus in the boiling water and simmer until it begins to curl, about 3 minutes. Remove from the heat and drain well. Slice the body and tentacles into 1 x 2$^1/_2$-in (2 x 6-cm) strips.

2 Using the tip of a knife, score the surface of the squid in a crisscross pattern to prevent it from over curling during cooking. Slice the squid into bite-sized pieces.

3 Thread the seafood pieces, alternating with the bell pepper and mushroom pieces, onto the skewers. Set aside.

4 Combine the Chili Paste Sauce ingredients in a bowl and mix well. Brush the seafood kebabs with the sauce on both sides until well coated.

5 Heat a little oil in a nonstick skillet or pan grill over medium heat. Cook the kebabs, a few at a time for 1–2 minutes on each side, taking care not to burn them. Remove from the heat, arrange on serving platters and serve hot with steamed rice.

Shrimp and Beef Salad

8 large fresh shrimp, rinsed well
8 oz (250 g) beef
Water to cover
1 zucchini or Japanese cucumber, halved and sliced
Salt
4 oz (125 g) cooked bamboo shoots, thickly sliced
Pinch of ground white pepper
1 tablespoon oil

Pine Nut Dressing
4 tablespoons dry-roasted ground pine nuts
$1/4$ cup (60 ml) beef stock
1 teaspoon salt, or to taste
2 teaspoons sesame oil
Pinch of ground white pepper

1 Place the shrimp in a heat-proof dish and steam in a steamer or covered wok over rapidly boiling water for 7–8 minutes. Remove from the heat and cool. Remove and discard the heads of the shrimp, peel and devein, then slice each shrimp into thirds. Set aside.
2 Place the beef in a saucepan, add enough of water to cover and bring to a boil over high heat. Reduce the heat to low, simmer uncovered for about 30 minutes and remove from the heat. Remove the beef from the stock and slice thinly. Reserve the beef stock for the Pine Nut Dressing.
3 Sprinkle the zucchini or cucumber slices with a pinch of salt and set aside for 10 minutes, then squeeze out any excess water from the zucchini or cucumber.
4 Sprinkle the bamboo shoot slices with a pinch of salt and pepper, and set aside for 5 minutes. Heat the oil in a skillet and sauté the bamboo slices for 1–2 minutes. Remove from the heat and drain on paper towels.
5 Combine the shrimp, beef and vegetables in a mixing bowl. Mix the Pine Nut Dressing ingredients together, then pour the dressing over the ingredients in the mixing bowl. Toss the salad until well blended, transfer to serving bowls and serve immediately.

Serves 4

Octopus or Squid with Hot Sauce and Noodles

10 oz (300 g) octopus or squid bodies
10 oz (300 g) dried wheat noodles (*somyeon*)
1¹/₂ tablespoons oil
10 fresh or canned button mushrooms, halved
1 green onion, cut into short lengths
1 red chili pepper, deseeded and cut into thin strips
1 onion, thinly sliced

Sauce
2 tablespoons Korean hot bean paste (*gochujang*)
2 tablespoons Korean chili powder
1 tablespoon crushed garlic paste
1 tablespoon minced green onion
2 teaspoons soy sauce
1 teaspoon sugar
¹/₂ teaspoon salt, or to taste
¹/₄ teaspoon freshly ground black pepper
2 tablespoons sesame oil
2 teaspoons sesame paste

1 Prepare the octopus or squid bodies as described on page 85. Set aside.

2 Bring a saucepan of water to a boil and blanch the noodles, stirring to prevent the noodles from sticking together, until soft, 3–5 minutes. Remove from the heat, rinse in cold water and drain well. Divide the noodles equally among 4 serving platters.

3 Combine the Sauce ingredients in a bowl and mix well. Set aside.

4 Heat the oil in a wok over high heat and stir-fry the vegetables for about 1 minute. Add the Sauce, mix well and bring to a boil. Add the octopus or squid and stir-fry for 1–2 minutes. Remove from the heat and spread equally over the noodles. Serve immediately.

Serves 4

Honey Dates (Daechucho)

20 fresh or dried dates, pitted, rinsed
$^1/_2$ cup (125 ml) rice wine
4 tablespoons pine nuts
$^1/_2$ cup (125 ml) honey

Serves 4

1 If using dried dates, soak the dates in the rice wine for 3 hours to soften. Omit this step if using fresh dates.
2 Insert 2 or 3 pine nuts into the opening of each date, allowing some nuts to protrude.
3 Drizzle a little honey over the dates and place the dates in a saucepan. Pour in the remaining honey and simmer the mixture over low heat, stirring, until the dates turn black. Remove from the heat. Arrange the dates, pine nut side up, on serving platters and serve.

Sweet Rice Pancakes (Hwajeon)

2 cups (250 g) sticky (glutinous) rice flour
4 tablespoons hot water
$^1/_2$ teaspoon salt
2 tablespoons oil
4 dates, pitted, thinly sliced
Edible flower petals and leaves, to garnish
$^1/_4$ cup (60 ml) honey, for brushing

Makes about 10

1 Combine the sticky (glutinous) rice flour, water and salt in a large bowl and mix into a soft dough, then knead with your hands for 10 minutes. On a lightly floured surface, roll out the dough to $^1/_3$ in (8 mm) thick. Using a cookie cutter or drinking glass, cut out 2-in (5-cm) circles.
2 Heat 1 teaspoon of the oil over medium heat in a nonstick skillet until hot, tilting the pan to coat the sides. Fry the dough circle, a few at a time, for 2–3 minutes, until transparent. Turn the rice cakes over and decorate the surface with sliced dates, flower petals and leaves. Continue frying for 1–2 more minutes and remove from the heat. Brush the rice cakes with honey when they are still hot. Serve warm.

Omija Berry Punch (Omijacha)

1/2 cup (20 g) dried
schizandra (*omija*)
berries
2 cups (500 ml) water
1/2 pear (preferably nashi),
peeled, cored and cut
into decorative pieces
1 teaspoon pine nuts
Salt, to taste (optional)

Sugar Syrup
3 cups (750 ml) water
1 cup (200 g) sugar

1 Wash the dried berries and soak them in the water overnight. Strain and discard the berries, reserve the strained liquid.

2 Make the Sugar Syrup by bringing the sugar and water to a boil in a saucepan, then simmer over low heat, stirring until the sugar is dissolved. Remove from the heat and set aside to cool.

3 Combine the strained liquid and Sugar Syrup and mix well. To serve, ladle into serving bowls or glasses and garnish with the pear pieces and some pine nuts. Add a pinch of salt if the drink tastes too sour.

Serves 4

Rice and Malt Drink (Sikhye)

1/2 cup (125 g) powdered
malt
6 cups (1 1/2 liters) water
1 cup (100 g) cooked rice
5 ginger slices
1/2 cup (100 g) sugar, or
to taste
1 teaspoon pine nuts, to
serve

Serves 4

1 In a saucepan, soak the malt in the water for 1 hour, then bring to a boil over high heat. Reduce the heat to low and simmer uncovered for about 30 minutes. Remove from the heat and strain through a fine sieve. Discard the solids and reserve the malt liquid.

2 Add the cooked rice to the malt liquid, stir well and set aside in a warm place until the rice floats to the surface, 3–4 hours. Strain the mixture and reserve the liquid. Rinse the rice grains well, cover and chill in the refrigerator.

3 Add the ginger slices and sugar to the strained liquid and bring to a boil in a saucepan, then simmer uncovered over low heat, stirring to dissolve the sugar, for about 10 minutes. Remove from the heat, discard the ginger slices and cool, then chill the malt tea in the refrigerator. To serve, ladle the chilled malt tea into serving bowls or cups, and top with some chilled rice grains and pine nuts.

Nashi Pear Dessert (Baesuk)

2 in (5 cm) fresh ginger
root, peeled and sliced
8 cups (2 liters) water
1 large nashi or other
firm pear
1 teaspoon black pepper-
corns
3/4 cup (150 g) sugar, or
to taste
1 tablespoon pine nuts

Serves 4–6

1 Bring the ginger and water to a boil in a pot and simmer uncovered for about 10 minutes. Remove from the heat. Strain the ginger water into a large saucepan and discard the ginger slices.

2 Peel and core the pear, then slice it into disks. Stud 3–5 black peppercorns into the edges of each disk, pressing them in firmly so they do not fall out during cooking.

3 Add the pear disks and sugar to the ginger water and simmer uncovered over medium heat until soft, 5–10 minutes. Remove the pear disks from the saucepan and set aside to cool.

4 To serve, ladle 1 cup (250 ml) of the ginger syrup into individual serving bowls, add 1–2 pear disks and sprinkle some pine nuts on top.

Dried Persimmon Punch (Sujeonggwa)

2 in (5 cm) fresh ginger root, peeled and sliced
6 cups (1 1/2 liters) water
1–2 cinnamon sticks
1/2 cup (100 g) sugar, or to taste
4 small or 2 medium dried seedless persimmons, stems trimmed, sliced into triangles
Pine nuts, to serve

1 Bring the ginger, water and cinnamon to a boil in a large saucepan. Reduce the heat to low and simmer uncovered for about 30 minutes. Add the sugar and stir until the sugar is dissolved. Remove from the heat and strain. Discard the solids.
2 Add the persimmon tringles to the cinnamon and ginger water 3 hours before serving to allow them to soften. Ladle to individual serving bowls, sprinkle some pine nuts on top and serve.

Serves 4

Complete List of Recipes